Marilyn J. Woody

WHY DID GOD MAKE ANGELS?

Illustrated by: Scott Holladay

Chariot Victor Publishing
A Division of Cook Communications

Dedication

To my precious grandchildren—
Jennifer, Katie, Alisha, and Jeremiah.
May God's mighty angel helpers
comfort and encourage.

M.W.

Chariot Victor Publishing,
a division of Cook Communications, Colorado Springs, Colorado 80918
Cook Communications, Paris, Ontario
Kingsway Communications, Eastbourne, England

WHY DID GOD MAKE ANGELS?
© 1992, 1999 by Marilyn J. Woody for text and Scott Holladay for illustrations.

Designed by Thomason Design Center

Scriptures are taken from the *Holy Bible: New International Version*®. © 1973, 1978, 1984
by the International Bible Society. Used by permission of Zondervan Bible Publishers.

First printing, 1999
Printed in Singapore
03 02 01 00 99   5 4 3 2 1

Previously published as *A Child's Book of Angels.*

As children read and hear these biblical accounts about God's helpers, they may ask, "What do angels really look like?" Illustrators through the ages have drawn their ideas, but the Bible gives only a few details. The important thing is the comforting reality of their existence and ability to minister to all who love God. Come along with me and learn about these majestic beings of God's creation.

Have you ever felt the warm sun on your face or the wind blowing your hair? Have you heard the birds singing and seen the brightly colored flowers? These are all ways that God's beautiful world sends Him praise.

In heaven, special angels called cherubim and seraphim are always worshiping and praising God. The seraphim sing, "Holy, holy, holy is the Lord Almighty; the whole earth is full of his glory."

God loves to hear *you* sing and pray, too. It makes Him happy when you think about Him. When you first wake up, when you go to bed, or any time during the day, you can just tell Him, "I sure do love you, God."

(Story taken from Isaiah 6:1-6; Ezekiel 10)

Dear God,
I want to praise You, too, like the seraphim and cherubim.
The whole world is full of Your glory!

6

"Last night an angel
of the God whose I
am and whom I
serve stood beside
me and said, 'Do
not be afraid,
Paul.' "
Acts 27:23, 24

Do you ever feel afraid? Sometimes even big, strong men get scared. That's what happened in this story.

A follower of Jesus named Paul was on a ship with many other men. As they sailed along, wild winds began to blow, and the ship creaked and groaned. The sky turned black, and the men couldn't see the sun or stars. For fourteen days, they had no food to eat.

They were so frightened. *Perhaps we will die*, they thought.

Then an angel came to Paul in the night and said, "Do not be afraid. You and everyone else on the ship will live."

Imagine how surprised and happy Paul was to hear that angel's good news!

We know that God is always watching over us. When we're in danger and afraid, He may even send His angel helpers to protect us.

(Story taken from Acts 27:13-44)

*Dear God,
Sometimes I get really scared. Help me to trust You when I'm afraid.*

8

Sometimes God uses His angels as mail carriers to deliver special messages. In this story, the angels looked just like ordinary people.

One day a man named Abraham saw three men coming toward his tent-home. They had been traveling and were tired and hungry. Abraham and his wife, Sarah, fixed them a picnic to eat under the trees.

Then one of the men said to Abraham, "Next year Sarah will have a son."

Abraham was amazed at this news. He was almost a hundred years old, and Sarah was ninety. Why, they were old enough to be grandparents, not a new mom and dad!

"Is anything too hard for the Lord?" one of the men asked Abraham.

Later, Abraham found out that the men were really angels. God had sent them to bring the happy announcement about the baby.

Perhaps you have seen an angel, too, and never even knew it! When you and your family are kind to homeless, sick, or hungry people, you may be helping an angel. You never know!

(Story taken from Genesis 18:1-15)

10

Dear God,
Help me to be kind and loving to people I meet.

Elijah was a prophet—a man sent by God to tell people how to live. He loved God with all his heart. When he saw people kneeling and praying to statues of wood or stone, he got very angry. He told them, "It is wrong to bow down to idols. You should pray only to God."

A bad queen named Jezebel told Elijah she would kill him for telling people about the one, true God. Elijah ran from Jezebel until he was so tired he fell asleep under a tree.

Then an angel came and touched Elijah. "Get up!" the angel said.

Elijah was surprised. He found hot baked bread and a jar of cool water. After he ate, he had so much energy he didn't get hungry again for forty days!

God knows when you feel worried and lonely, too. Isn't it comforting to think about all the ways He helps us? When His servant Elijah was in need, God even sent an angel.

(Story taken from I Kings 19:1-8)

"Then [Elijah] lay down under the tree and fell asleep. All at once an angel touched him and said, 'Get up and eat.' "
I Kings 19:5

Dear God,
The Bible says God has thousands of angels. I'm glad such a great God never leaves me alone.

P eter was arrested and put in prison because he loved Jesus and told other people about Him. He was guarded there by two soldiers. While Peter sat in his prison cell, his friends prayed that he would be set free soon. Guess what happened.

The night before Peter was to stand before the king who had put him in prison, an angel suddenly appeared to him. A bright light filled Peter's cell, and Peter felt a tap on his side.

"Quick, get up!" said the angel. The chains fell off Peter's wrists. "Put your clothes on, Peter, and follow me."

Peter never got dressed so fast in all his life!

The angel opened the prison gates, and he and Peter walked right past the sleeping guards!

Even when things look very bad, God knows what's happening. He hears when you pray, and He may use His angels to help answer your prayers.

(Story taken from Acts 12:1-19)

". . . Peter was sleeping between two soldiers, bound with two chains, and sentries stood guard at the entrance. Suddenly an angel of the Lord appeared and a light shone in the cell."
Acts 12:6,7

Dear God,
Help me to be faithful to You like Peter was. Thank You for hearing me when I pray.

14

Have you ever gone to the zoo? The powerful lions are fun to see, but not to touch! They are kept in big caves with fences around them so they cannot hurt you.

But once a man named Daniel got very close to some hungry lions. Daniel loved God with all his heart. His king wanted people to bow down and worship him, but Daniel wouldn't. Three times a day, Daniel knelt and prayed to God.

So the king made a rule that people must pray to him or be put in the den with hungry lions. Daniel knew he should only pray to God, no matter what the king said. So, sure enough, he ended up with the lions.

But—surprise!—God sent an angel to shut the lions' mouths! The next morning, when the king came to look, he found that Daniel didn't even have a scratch!

You and I never need to be embarrassed about praying to God, no matter what. We must remember that all the angels of heaven are on the side of those who love and obey God.

(Story taken from Daniel 6)

16 *Dear God,*
Help me to be proud of You like Daniel. I want everyone to know I love You.

We live in a world where both good and bad happen.

Every day we hear news about wrong things people do. Another story about Daniel will help you understand why this is true.

Daniel felt very sad about all the bad things he saw happening. He talked to God and told Him how sorry he was for the wicked things people were doing.

Later, an angel named Gabriel flew swiftly to him.

"Do not be afraid, Daniel," said Gabriel. "I would have come even faster, but for twenty-one days I had to fight the prince of Persia. Another angel, Michael, helped me win the battle."

Imagine! God has strong warrior angels in the heavens, fighting against the evil angels of Satan's kingdom—guarding us from the evil one.

What do you think you would see if the sky were folded back? More angels than you could count, helping to protect you!

(Story taken from Daniel 9 and 10)

Dear God,
18 *You love me so much You have angels who can keep me from evil. Help me always to remember that.*

Imagine the longest ladder you have ever seen. Maybe it was on a fire truck that had a driver in the front and back. The ladder in this story is even longer than that.

Jacob was away from home on a trip and was very tired. He had just gone to sleep and was dreaming. In his dream, he saw angels going up and down a long, long ladder that reached all the way from earth to heaven.

God was at the top of the ladder. He told Jacob, "I will protect you wherever you go."

When Jacob woke up, he knew God had talked to him.

God used His angels to help Jacob not to be afraid. When you put your head on your soft pillow at night, remember that God's angels are watching over you, too.

(Story taken from Genesis 28:10-22)

Dear God,
Instead of just talking to Jacob from heaven, You used a ladder and angels. What a good idea! Even if You don't send angels to me in my dreams, I know You're watching over me.

20

When you go on a trip with your family, you need a map. It shows you which roads to take and where to turn.

The people in this picture were going on a trip. A man named Moses was their leader. His job was to take them from Egypt to their new home—but he didn't have a map. Instead, God sent an angel to guide and protect them!

God told the people to listen to the angel. If they obeyed, they would be safe. And since angels never get tired, the people would be watched over night and day. With an angel to guide them, Moses and the people didn't need a map.

God still uses His angels today. Close your eyes and try to imagine all the places they might be.

(Story taken from 23:20-33)

"See, I am sending an angel ahead of you to guard you along the way and to bring you to the place I have prepared."
Exodus 23:20

Dear God,
I'm thankful Your angel helpers never sleep. I want to be Your helper, too.

22

od has thousands and thousands of angels to help Him. The angel Gabriel has a special job of delivering important messages.

The most important message Gabriel ever delivered was to a young woman named Mary. He told her she was going to have a baby—Jesus! God had chosen her to be the mother of His Son.

This was the best news that had ever come from heaven to earth! Because Jesus, God's Son, came to save us from our sins. The world would never be the same again.

"Do not be afraid," Gabriel said to Mary.

And when you have Jesus in your heart, you do not need to be afraid, either.

(Story taken from Luke 1:26-38)

Dear God,
I'm glad You sent Gabriel to tell Mary the good news about Jesus.
Thank You that Jesus helps me when I am afraid.

"But the angel said to her, 'Do not be afraid, Mary, you have found favor with God. You will be with child and give birth to a son, and you are to give him the name Jesus."
Luke 1:30-31

24

When you were born, everyone was excited. Grandmas, grandpas, friends and neighbors all came to look at you—the new baby!

When Baby Jesus was born, he had lots of visitors, too . . . but none were his grandpa or grandma. Jesus' mother, Mary, was far from home when he was born.

The inn was full, and there was no hospital in Bethlehem. Jesus was born in a stable with sleeping cows and sheep. So Mary and Joseph were very surprised to hear from the shepherds that the heavens had been full of singing angels.

Yes, when God wanted a giant celebration for Jesus' birth, He called on His wonderful angel helpers. Baby Jesus, God's Son, had so many angels to praise him that only the sky could hold them!

(Story taken from Luke 2:1-20)

Dear God,
I wish I could have been there the night Jesus was born, and seen the sky full of Your singing angels! I'm happy that Jesus came to earth, too. I want to sing praises like the angels!

"Suddenly a great company of the heavenly host appeared with the angel, praising God and saying, 'Glory to God in the highest, and on earth peace to men on whom his favor rests.'"
Luke 2:13-14

26

When Jesus was on earth, He told lots of stories to His friends. One day while He and His helpers were eating dinner, Jesus said, "A woman who had ten silver coins lost one."

(That would be like having ten shiny dimes and losing one of them in your bedroom.)

"She took a light, swept the house and looked carefully until she found it. Then she called her friends and neighbors together and said, 'Rejoice with me, I have found my lost coin.' "

Jesus told this story so we would understand how much He loves us. We are worth more to Him than all the money in the world.

When someone on earth asks Jesus into his or her heart, the angels get so excited they have a celebration. See how happy the angels in this picture look? Have they had a party for you?

(Story taken from Luke 15:8-10)

Dear God,
Thank You for loving me so much. I'm glad Your angels had a big
party when I asked Jesus into my heart.

"... I tell you, there is rejoicing in the presence of the angels of God over one sinner who repents."
Luke 15:10

28

Faith Parenting Guide

AGE: 4-7

LIFE ISSUE: My child doesn't understand who angels are
and how they help God take care of us.

VALUE: Bible Knowledge/Faith

Learning Styles

VISUAL LEARNING STYLE: Have your child choose a favorite story from this book and draw his or her
own picture of that scene on a piece of paper. Discuss what part the angel(s) played in the story.
Then discuss how this can relate to helping your child in his or her everyday life.

AUDITORY LEARNING STYLE: Read the story of Abraham, Jacob, Moses and the Ten Commandments,
Elijah, Daniel, Mary, Peter's escape from prison, and Paul's shipwreck from another Bible storybook.
Talk about how important it was for the angel to obey God's instructions.
How can we be special messengers for God today?

TACTILE LEARNING STYLE: Set up an obstacle course inside or outside your house. This can be
as elaborate as you want it to be or as simple as a few chairs and tables scattered throughout the room.
Blindfold your child. You'll need to recruit an older brother or sister, friend, or even a spouse to help
your child navigate the course. First, let your child try to get through the obstacle course with no guidance.
Then tell you helper to safely guide the child through the course. Ask the child: What would have happened if
you didn't have someone to help you? When I told the helper to guide you, how was that like God telling angels
to help you? How can angels help you just like your helper guided you through the obstacle course today?

The Bible is the only book that tells us for sure what we can know about angels and whatever we read
should always be compared with that. Scriptures that tell us about angels are:

Exodus 23:20	Psalm 91:11	Matthew 18:10	Luke 15:10	Acts 27:23, 24
1 Kings 19:5-7	Psalm 103:20	Mark 1:13	Luke 22:43	Hebrews 1:14
Job 38:7	Ezekiel 10:4	Luke 1:30, 31	Acts 7:53	Hebrews 13:2
Psalm 34:7	Daniel 6:22	Luke 2:13, 14	Acts 12:6-11	